WORK FROM HOME DIRECTORY

	COMPANY	Status	HOW TO APPLY
1	ACCOUNTING	CURRENT	http://www.bookminders.com
2		CURRENT	http://www.balancyourbooks.com/jobs.shtml
3		CURRENT	http://www.fastebart.com/about/careers
4		CURRENT	http://www.tadaccounting.com/Original/Careers.html
5		CURRENT	http://www.batemanhouston.com/employme_.htm
6		CURRENT	http://www.cieLayouts.com/whoweare_careers.html
7		CURRENT	http://ignitespot.com/small-business-accountant/careers
8		CURRENT	http://www.invsql.com/about/jobs
9		CURRENT	
10		CURRENT	http://advisetech.com/company-at/career-opportunities
11		CURRENT	http://www.driverguide.com
12		CURRENT	http://www.dielsyoufone-company/media-_center
13		CURRENT	http://www.teletechjobs.com/athome-en-US
14		CURRENT	http://www.apply.westathome.com/index.htm

CALLCENTER AGENCIES
www.theonlinebusiness.com
callcenter.liveops.com (www.liveops.com)
www.westathome.com
www.workingsol.com
www.accoladesupport.com
www.customloyal.com
www.sciathome.com
www.repsforrent.com
www.overflowusa.com
http://abcnews.go.com/gma/takecontrolofyourlife
www.acddirect.com
www.alpineaccess.com

ACCOUNTING & BOOKKEEPING
www.clickaccounts.com

www.clicknwork.com
www.bookminders.com
www.osibusinessservices.com
DATA ENTRY
www.workingsol.com
www.keyforcash.com
www.absolutedocs.com/career
www.accutranglobal.com
www.axiondata.com
www.captioncolorado.com
www.driverguide.com
www.fdch.com/careers
www.mulberrystudio.com
www.reedtech.com
www.tdec.com
www.tigerfish.com/employment.html

ADMINISTRATIVE / TRANSCRIPTION
www.accentance.com
www.aldersonreporting.com
www.eventranscription.com
www.moderndayscribe.com
www.mountainwestprocessing.com
www.teamdoubleclick.com
www.eCallogy.com
www.accuratetyping.net/atsiempl.html
CUSTOMER SERVICE / TELECOMMUNICATIONS
www.accoladesupport.com
www.acddirect.com

www.alpineaccess.com
www.auralog.com
www.channelblend.com
www.cloud10corp.com
www.customloyal.com
www.hirepoint.com
www.ictgroup.com
www.liveops.com
www.onpointathome.com
www.scilive.com
www.securecallmanagement.com
www.service800.com
www.telcare.com
www.verafast.com/job_opportunities.htm
www.vipdesk.com
www.bsgcleaning.com/voicelogthirdpartyverification
www.westathome.com
www.westat.com
www.myxact.com
www.arise.com

WRITING / EDITING / PROOF-READING
www.associatedcontent.com
www.helium.com
www.mylot.com
www.guru.com
www.writingassist.com
www.writersweekly.com
www.proofreadnow.com
www.myessays.com
www.cyberedit.com
www.sunoasis.com
www.examiner.com
www.telerepsathome.com
www.partnerwithpaul.com
www.theonlinebusiness.com

WORK FROM HOME SEARCH SITES
www.workathomedesk.com/directory
www.workathome-authority.com
www.nextjobathome.com
www.oDesk.com
www.craigslist.com
www.eLance.com
www.simplyhired.com
www.classifiedads.com/search
www.about.com/search
www.workathomemoms.about.com
www.aarp.com/search
www.wahm.com/directories/wahm-businesses
www.wahm.com/business-opportunities
FEE BASED WORK FROM HOME SEARCH SITES

www.profitwebsystem.com
www.homejobstop.com
www.telerepsathome.com
www.online-home-careers.com
www.paidsurveysandmore.net
www.wahuniversity.com
GET PAID TO COMPLETE SURVEYS
www.ipsos.com
us.lightspeedpanel.com
www.globaltestmarket.com
www.toluna.com
www.greenfieldonline.com
www.mindfieldonline.com
www.sendearnings.com

www.memolink.com

en-us.nielsen.com

WORK FROM HOME DIRECTORY

	COMPANY	Status	HOW TO APPLY
1	DATA ENTRY	Current	https://www.fancyhands.com/jobs
2		Current	https://www.virtual.com
3		Current	https://scribie.com/freelance-transcription#intro
4		Current	http://my365assistant.com
5		Current	http://www.clickworker.com/become-a-clickworker/?utm_source=456653&utm_campaign=CW4CW&utm_medium=email
6		Current	https://www.capitaltyping.com
7		Current	http://www.diondatasolutions.net/opportunities.htm
8		Current	http://www.tdec.com/contact-us/jobs-opportunities
9		Current	http://www.axiondata.com
10		Current	https://speakwrite.com
11		Current	http://support.crowdsource.com/support/home?referer=cloudcrowd
12		Current	http://siciwrite.com/careers/index.ap
13		Current	https://workers.virtualbee.com
14		Current	http://asiuzdataing.com
15		Current	http://www.flexjobs.com/jobs/telecommuting-jobs-at-driverguide.com

MASTER WORK FROM HOME DIRECTORY LIST

	COMPANY	Status	HOW TO APPLY
1	CRUISE.COM	CALL CENTER	ON-LINE
2	DRIVERGUIDE.COM	DATA ENTRY	ON-LINE
3	INTUIT.COM	CPAs - TAX ATTORNEY	ON-LINE
4	JETBLUE.COM	CALL CENTER	ON-LINE
5	MEDCO.COM	CALL CENTER	ON-LINE
6	MEDIFAX.COM	TRANSCRIPTION	ON-LINE
7	NETMED.COM	TRANSCRIPTION	ON-LINE
8	MRECORD.COM	MEDICAL CODING	ON-LINE
9	https://www.newcorp.com/	CALL CENTER	ON-LINE
10	THE NEWTON GROUP	APPOINTMENT SETTIN	ON-LINE
11	QUEST DIAGNOSTICS	TELE INTERVIEWS	ON-LINE
12	QUICK TATE	DATA ENTRY	ON-LINE
13	SCRIBE	DATA ENTRY	ON-LINE
14	SMART OFFICE SOL	SALES - MARKETING	ON-LINE
15	SPEAK WRITE	DATA ENTRY	ON-LINE
16	SYLVAN LEARNING	TEACHING	ON-LINE
17	TELENETWORK	CALL CENTER	ON-LINE
18	TELETECH	CALL CENTER	ON-LINE
19	TERMINIX	CALL CENTER	ON-LINE
20	TRANSCEND SERVICES	TRANSCRIPTION	ON-LINE
21	TRANS TECH	TRANSCRIPTION	ON-LINE
22	VITAC	TRANSCRIPTION	ON-LINE
23	WEBMAX	TRANSCRIPTION	ON-LINE
24	UBIQUS	TRANSCRIPTION	ON-LINE
25	UHAUL	CALL CENTER	ON-LINE
26	VER-A-FAST	CALL CENTER	ON-LINE
27	VIP DESK	CALL CENTER	ON-LINE
28	VIRTUAL BEE	DATA ENTRY	ON-LINE
29	VIRTUAL RADIOLOGIC	TELERADIOLOGY - DR.	ON-LINE
30	WELL POINT	NURSING - CASE MGT	ON-LINE
31	COUNSEL ON CALL	ATTORNEY - PARALEGAL	ON-LINE
32	COURSEBRIDGE	INSTRUCTORS	ON-LINE
33	CONIFER HEALTH SOL	NURSING	ON-LINE
34	COVANCE	NURSING	ON-LINE
35	COX COMMUNICATION	CALL CENTER	ON-LINE
36	I-HIRE NATIONAL	VIRTUAL RECRUITER	ON-LINE
37	FAHT	CALL CENTER	ON-LINE
38	WCD	MILITARY MOMS W@H	ON-LINE
39	ASURION	CALL CENTER	ON-LINE
40	BALANCE STAFFING	TECHNICAL SUPPORT	ON-LINE
41	TEAM TAYLOR, INC.	CALL CENTER INBOUND	ON-LINE
42	WORKATHOMEDESK.COM	W@H JOB DIRECTORIES	ON-LINE
43	BSG	3RD PARTY VERICATION	ON-LINE
44	CAPITAL TYPING	DATA ENTRY, TRANSCRIPTION, CALL	ON-LINE

		CENTER	
45	CCI	CALL CENTER BILINGUAL	ON-LINE
46	CENTURY LINK	CALL CENTER	ON-LINE
47	ABOUT.COM	WORK@HOME JOBS AND COMPANIES	ON-LINE DIRECTORIES
48	DIRECTSELLING411.COM	HOME BUSINESS KITS - CONSULTANT	ON-LINE
49	ISHIRING.ME	WORK@HOME	ON-LINE SEARCH
50	MONSTER.COM	WORK@HOME	ON-LINE SEARCH
51	INDEED.COM	WORK@HOME	ON-LINE SEARCH
52	SIMPLYHIRED.COM	WORK@HOME	ON-LINE SEARCH
53	STITCHFIX.COM	CLOTHING ACCORDING TO PROFILE	ON-LINE
54	FASHION GROUP, INC.	CREATE OWN CLOTHING LINE	212*463*0800
55	ARGYLEPARTNERS.COM	CREATE OWN CLOTHING LINE	323*330*9515
56	YELP.COM	WORK@HOME	ON-LINE SEARCH
57	DUCKDUCKGO.COM	WORK@HOME	ON-LINE SEARCH
58	WAHM.COM	WORK@HOME "EXCELLENT SOURCE"	DIRECTORY LISTINGS
59	DSA.ORG	DIRECT SELLING ASSOCIATION	DIRECT SELLING DIR.
60	BIZYMOMS.COM	WORK@HOME	DIRECTORIES
61	HBWM.COM	WORK@HOME	DIRECTORIES
62	FEMALECREATIONS.COM	WORK@HOME	DIRECTORIES
63	INTERNETBASEDMOMS.COM	WORK@HOME	DIRECTORIES
64	MYDSWA.ORG	DIRECT SELLING	DIRECTORIES
65	BUSINESSOWNERSIDEACAFE.COM	WORK@HOME	DIRECTORIES
66	MOMPACK.COM	WORK@HOME	DIRECTORIES
67	FRANCHISESOLUTIONS.COM	FRANCHISE - VENDING	DIRECTORIES
68	ALPINE ACCESS	CALL CENTER	ON-LINE
69	AT&T	CALL CENTER	ON-LINE
70	WEST-AT-HOME	CALL CENTER	ON-LINE
71	WORKING SOLUTIONS	CALL CENTER	ON-LINE
72	ARISE.COM	CALL CENTER	ON-LINE
73	ACD DIRECT	SALES - CUSTOMER SERVICE	ON-LINE
74	LIVEOPS.COM	SALES - CUSTOMER SERVICE	ON-LINE
75	CLOUD10CORP.COM	CALL CENTER	ON-LINE
76	CONVERGYS.COM	CALL CENTER	ON-LINE
77	HIRE POINT	CALL CENTER	ON-LINE
78	ACCOLADE SUPPORT	CALL CENTER	http://www.accoladesupport.com/techjob.html
79	EBAY PROFIT	EMAIL PROCESSOR	ON-LINE
80	VITACOST.COM	EMAIL CUSTOMER SUPPORT SPECIALST	ON-LINE
81	THE HOLTZ GROUP	EMAIL PROCESSOR	ON-LINE
82	MEDICAL-OCCUPATIONAL HEALTH CONSULTANTS, PSC	TRANSCRIPTION	ON-LINE
83	WOODWARD	WORK@HOME	ON-LINE SEARCH

84	DAILY MONEY TEAM	W@HOME RECEPTIONIST	ON-LINE
85	SYKES HOME	CALL CENTER	ON-LINE
86	DMT INBOUND	CALL CENTER	ON-LINE
87	DMT ADVERTISING	CALL CENTER	ON-LINE
88	ELITE WORK AT HOME	CALL CENTER REPS	ON-LINE
89	SDS APPOINTMENTS - odesk.com	APPOINTMENT SETTING	ON-LINE
90	IRVINE TECHNOLOGY CORP	VERINT CALL RECORDING MONITOR	ON-LINE
91	CONVERGYS	CALL CENTER	ON-LINE
92	HOME FRONT HEROES	VIRTUAL CALL CENTER	ON-LINE
93	WAHE.COM	RETIRED INSURANCE AGENTS	ON-LINE
94	EMPLOYMENT CONNECTION	WORK@HOME - VIRTUAL AGENTS	DIRECTORIES
95	2WORKONLINE.COM	DATA ENTRY	ON-LINE
96	CONFIDENTIAL COMPANY	ADMINISTRATIVE	ON-LINE
97	ENTERPRISE	RESERVATION CSR	VIRTUAL
98	UHAUL	RESERVATION CSR	VIRTUAL
99	JOB-FRENZY.COM	WORK@HOME	ON-LINE SEARCH
100	EMPLOYMENTGUIDE.COM	WORK@HOME	ON-LINE SEARCH
101	JOBS-ATHOME.NET	WORK@HOME	ON-LINE SEARCH
102	CAREERBUILDER.COM	WORK@HOME	ON-LINE SEARCH
103	LINKEDIN.COM	WORK@HOME	ON-LINE SEARCH
104	SNAGAJOB.COM	WORK@HOME	ON-LINE SEARCH
105	THELADDERS.COM	WORK@HOME	ON-LINE SEARCH
106	BRIDGESPAN.ORG	WORK@HOME	ON-LINE SEARCH
107	CAREERONESTOP.ORG	WORK@HOME	ON-LINE SEARCH
108	BBB.ORG/BLOG	WORK@HOME	ON-LINE SEARCH
109	AXION DATA	DATA ENTRY	ON-LINE
110	DION DATA SOLUTIONS	DATA ENTRY	ON-LINE
111	KEY FOR CASH	DATA ENTRY	ON-LINE
112	MYSTERYSHOP.ORG	MYSTERY SHOPPING ASSOCIATION	ON-LINE DIRECTORY
113	ECALLOGY.COM	CALL CENTER	ON-LINE
114	MICAH TEK, INC.	CALL CENTER	ON-LINE
115	O'CURRANCE	CALL CENTER	ON-LINE
116	CUSTOMLOYAL.COM	CALL CENTER	ON-LINE
117	ON POINT AT HOME	CALL CENTER	ON-LINE
118	SCI LIVE	CALL CENTER	ON-LINE
119	SERVICE800.COM	CALL CENTER	ON-LINE
120	TELCARE	CALL CENTER	ON-LINE
121	TELEREACH	CALL CENTER	ON-LINE
122	TELEXPERTISE, INCL	CALL CENTER	ON-LINE
123	XACT TELESOLUTIONS	CALL CENTER	ON-LINE
124	ACCENTANCE.COM	TRANSCRIPTION	ON-LINE
125	ALDERSONREPORTING.COM	COURT TYPING	ON-LINE
126	PALM COAST DATA	DATA ENTRY KEYERS	ON-LINE
127	TEAMDOUBLECLICK.COM	VIRTUAL ASSISTANTS	ON-LINE

#	Site	Category	Status
128	CLICKACCOUNTS.COM	ACCOUNTING - FINANCE	ON-LINE
129	CLICKNWORK.COM	ACCOUNTING - FINANCE	ON-LINE
130	BOOKMINDERS.COM	ACCOUNTING - FINANCE	ON-LINE
131	OSIBUSINESSERVICES.COM	ACCOUNTING - FINANCE	ON-LINE
132	1800FLOWERS.COM	CALL CENTER	ON-LINE
133	ARO	CALL CENTER	ON-LINE
134	ASI	CALL CENTER	ON-LINE
135	GE "GENERAL ELECTRIC"	CALL CENTER	ON-LINE
136	SECURE CALL MANAGEMENT	CALL CENTER	ON-LINE
137	TIME COMMUNICATIONS	CALL CENTER	ON-LINE
138	VIRTUESERVE	CALL CENTER	ON-LINE
139	VOICE LOG	CALL CENTER	ON-LINE
140	STAFFMARK.COM	WORK@HOME - ASURION - NEW CORP	ON-LINE
141	ESCRIPTIONIST.COM	TRANSCRIPTION	ON-LINE
142	MEDQUIST.COM	TRANSCRIPTION RESOURCES - OPPS	ON-LINE
143	MTRECRUITERS.COM	TRANSCRIPTION	ON-LINE SEARCH
144	ORACLE TRANSCRIPTION.COM	TRANSCRIPTION	ON-LINE SEARCH
145	PRODUCTIONTRANSCRIPTS.COM	TRANSCRIPTION	ON-LINE SEARCH
146	TALK2TYPE.ET	TRANSCRIPTION	SEND RESUME TO: JOBS@TALK2TYPE.NET
147	TIGERFISH.COM	TRANSCRIPTION	ON-LINE
148	NUANCE.COM	TRANSCRIPTION	ON-LINE EMPLOYMENT SEARCH
149	TRANSCRIPTION-SERVICES.ORG	TRANSCRIPTION	ON-LINE SEARCH
150	WWW2.AXSMKTG.COM	WORK@HOME	ON-LINE SEARCH
151	INTELEMARK.COM	SALES AGENTS	ON-LINE
152	ELANCE.COM	WRITING	ON-LINE
153	WRITINGASSIST.COM	WRITING	ON-LINE
154	WRITERSWEEKLY.COM	WRITING	ON-LINE
155	PROOFREADNOW.COM	PROOFING - EDITING	ON-LINE
156	MYESSAY.COM	ACADEMIC WRITING	ON-LINE
157	CYBEREDIT.COM	PROOFING - EDITING	ON-LINE
158	SUNOASIS.COM	WRITING	ON-LINE
159	ASSOCIATEDCONTENT.COM	WRITING	ON-LINE
160	HELIUM.COM	WRITING	ON-LINE
161	GURU.COM	WRITING	ON-LINE
162	MYLOT.COM	WRITING	ON-LINE
163	SUNMAGAZINE.ORG	WRITING "EXCELLENT SOURCE"	ON-LINE
164	GETAFREELANCER.COM	WRITING	ON-LINE DIRECTORY
165	INTELLICARE.COM	CALL CENTER	ON-LINE
166	MSVAS.COM	VIRTUAL ASSISTANT	ON-LINE
167	WEST.COM	VIRTUAL AGENTS	ON-LINE
168	WORKPLACELIKEHOME.COM	DISCUSSION FORUM	WORK@HOME LEADS
169	CONSUMERFRAUDREPORTING.ORG	REPORT FRAUDS	SEARCH FOR

			LEGITIMATE WORK@HOME
170	CONSUMERSGUIDETOMAKINGMONEYO NLINE.ORG	SAFETY GUIDE	ON-LINE BUSINESS
171	BECOMEAGUIDE.CHACHA.COM	GUIDE	ON-LINE
172	http://www.a-closer-look.com/	MYSTERY SHOPPER	ON-LINE
173	SECOND-TO-NONE.COM	MYSTERY SHOPPER	ON-LINE
174	INTELLI-SHOP.COM	MYSTERY SHOPPER	ON-LINE
175	THEBRANDTGROUP.COM	MYSTERY SHOPPER	ON-LINE
176	STERICYCLEEXPERTSOLUTIONS.COM/S HOP	MYSTERY SHOPPER	ON-LINE
177	BESTMARK.COM	MYSTERY SHOPPER	ON-LINE
178	ISHOPFORYOU.COM	MYSTERY SHOPPER	ON-LINE
179	ACEMYSTERYSHOPPING.COM	MYSTERY SHOPPER	ON-LINE SEARCH
180	AMUSEMENTADVANTAGE.COM	MYSTERY SHOPPER	ON-LINE
181	http://www.asapittsburgh.com/	MYSTERY SHOPPER	ON-LINE
182	http://www.apartmentmysteryshopper.com/	APARTMENT SHOPPER	ON-LINE
183	https://www.ardentservices.com/	MYSTERY SHOPPER	ON-LINE
184	http://www.aysm.com/	MYSTERY SHOPPER	ON-LINE
185	http://www.barvinternational.com/	MYSTERY SHOPPER	ON-LINE
186	http://www.informars.com/main/default.aspx	MYSTERY SHOPPER	ON-LINE
187	http://www.mystery-shopping.com/	MYSTERY SHOPPER	ON-LINE
188	http://www.shopaudits.com/	MYSTERY SHOPPER	ON-LINE
189	http://www.marketforce.com/client-logins/	MYSTERY SHOPPER	ON-LINE
190	http://www.checkupmarketing.com/	MYSTERY SHOPPER	SEARCH DIRECTORY
191	http://www.consumerimpressions.com	MYSTERY SHOPPER	ON-LINE
192	http://www.crg2000.com/	MYSTERY SHOPPER	ON-LINE
193	http://audit.stericycleexpertsolutions.com/	MYSTERY SHOPPER	ON-LINE
194	http://www.ucpuntonus.com/	MYSTERY SHOPPER	ON-LINE
195	http://www.customerperspectives.com/	MYSTERY SHOPPER	ON-LINE
196	http://www.customerserviceexperts.com/	MYSTERY SHOPPER	ON-LINE
197	http://www.esperceptions.com/	MYSTERY SHOPPER	ON-LINE
198	http://www1.cv-market.com/	MYSTERY SHOPPER	SEARCH DIRECTORY
199	http://www.sparksresearch.com/	MYSTERY SHOPPER	ON-LINE
200	http://www.dsgai.com/	MYSTERY SHOPPER	ON-LINE
201	http://www.dunlapenterprises.com/	MYSTERY SHOPPER	ON-LINE
202	http://www.howardservices.com/index.php	MYSTERY SHOPPER	ON-LINE
203	http://ww2.imaginusinc.com/?folio=566258416 &bkt=9699	MYSTERY SHOPPER	ON-LINE SEARCH
204	http://www.shopperjobs.com/	MYSTERY SHOPPER	ON-LINE
205	https://www.secretshopper.com/	MYSTERY SHOPPER	ON-LINE

206	http://www.texasshoppersnetwork.com/	MYSTERY SHOPPER	ON-LINE
207	http://spiesindisguise.com/index/	MYSTERY SHOPPER	ON-LINE
208	http://www.ssanet.com/NewShoppers	MYSTERY SHOPPER	ON-LINE
209	http://www.servicetrac.com/	MYSTERY SHOPPER	ON-LINE
210	http://serviceresearch.com/	MYSTERY SHOPPER	ON-LINE
211	http://www.service-quality.com/	MYSTERY SHOPPER	ON-LINE
212	http://www.spgweb.com/	MYSTERY SHOPPER	ON-LINE
213	http://www.serviceevaluation.com/	MYSTERY SHOPPER	ON-LINE
214	http://www.servicecheck.com/	MYSTERY SHOPPER	ON-LINE
215	http://www.servicealliancinc.com/	MYSTERY SHOPPER	ON-LINE
216	http://www.sqm.ca/index.php/en/	MYSTERY SHOPPER	ON-LINE
217	http://www.secretshoppingservices.com	MYSTERY SHOPPER	ON-LINE
218	http://www.aboutfacecorp.com/ce_bis_shoptype_s.cfm	MYSTERY SHOPPER	ON-LINE
219	http://www.satisfactionservicesinc.com/	MYSTERY SHOPPER	ON-LINE
220	http://www.rqa-inc.com/na_home.html	MYSTERY SHOPPER	ON-LINE
221	http://www.rocksmm.com/	MYSTERY SHOPPER	ON-LINE
222	http://www.restaurantevaluators.com/	MYSTERY SHOPPER	ON-LINE
223	http://www.restaurant-cops.com/	MYSTERY SHOPPER	ON-LINE
224	http://www.remysteryshopper.com/	MYSTERY SHOPPER	ON-LINE
225	http://www.questforbest.com/	MYSTERY SHOPPER	ON-LINE
226	http://www.qsispecialists.com/	MYSTERY SHOPPER	ON-LINE
227	http://www.qacinc.com/	MYSTERY SHOPPER	ON-LINE
228	http://www.qams.com/	MYSTERY SHOPPER	ON-LINE
229	http://www.proreview.net/	MYSTERY SHOPPER	SEARCH DIRECTORY
230	http://www.premierservice.ca/	MYSTERY SHOPPER	NATIONWIDE
231	http://www.pedge.com/	MYSTERY SHOPPER	ON-LINE
232	http://www.pacificresearchgroup.com/	MYSTERY SHOPPER	ON-LINE
233	http://www.nylpc.com/	MYSTERY SHOPPER	ON-LINE
234	http://ww2.nationwidesg.com/?folio=435329566 &bkt=9657	MYSTERY SHOPPER	NATIONWIDE SEARCH
235	http://www.mysteryshopper.net/scam.asp	MYSTERY SHOPPER	SCAM ALERTS
236	http://www.mysteryshopper.net/	MYSTERY SHOPPER	ON-LINE
237	http://www.mystiqueshopper.com/	MYSTERY SHOPPER	ON-LINE
238	http://www.mystery-shoppers.com/	MYSTERY SHOPPER	ON-LINE
239	http://ww2.mercsurveys.com/?folio=780178153 &bkt=9697	MYSTERY SHOPPER	SEARCH DIRECTORY

#	URL	Category	Type
240	http://melindabrody.com/mystery-shopping/	MYSTERY SHOPPER	ON-LINE
241	http://www.marketviewpoint.com/	MYSTERY SHOPPER	ON-LINE
242	http://www.marsresearch.com/employment/	RESEARCH INTERVIEWER	ON-LINE
243	https://www.maritzmysteryshopping.com/home/Default.aspx	MYSTERY SHOPPER	ON-LINE
244	http://www.mleblanc.com/	MYSTERY SHOPPER	ON-LINE
245	http://www.kernscheduling.com/	MYSTERY SHOPPER	ON-LINE
246	http://www.satisfactionservicesinc.com/index2.html	MYSTERY SHOPPER	ON-LINE
247	http://www.shopyourway.com/app/LT?p=3_0%26sid%3dISm20140120x000074xPaidSearch	MYSTERY SHOPPER	ON-LINE
248	http://www.thepennyhoarder.com/best-mystery-shopping-companies-to-work/?gclid=COiXiv6px7wCFWwV7AodmUsA_Zg	MYSTERY SHOPPER	ON-LINE
249	http://www.marketforce.com/become-a-mystery-shopper/	MYSTERY SHOPPER	ON-LINE
250	http://www.sinclaircustomermetrics.com/	MYSTERY SHOPPER	ON-LINE
251	https://www.bestmark.com/become_a_shopper.htm?r=FL7420	MYSTERY SHOPPER	SEARCH DIRECTORY
252	http://www.jancyn.com/	MYSTERY SHOPPER	ON-LINE
253	http://www.jmridgway.com/	MYSTERY SHOPPER	ON-LINE
254	http://www.internationalservicecheck.com	MYSTERY SHOPPER	NATIONAL
255	http://www.intelli-shop.com/	MYSTERY SHOPPER	ON-LINE
256	http://www.infotelinc.com/	MYSTERY SHOPPER	SEARCH DIRECTORY
257	http://www.imyst.com/	MYSTERY SHOPPER	ON-LINE
258	http://www.trygsi.com/index.asp	HOME BUSINESS OPP	DIRECT SELLING
259	http://search.about.com/?q=work+from+home+jobs	WORK FROM HOME	SEARCH DIRECTORY
260	http://search.aarp.org/browse?Ntt=work+at+home+jobs	WORK FROM HOME	RETIREE DIRECTORY
261	http://www.ehow.com/search.html?s=work+at+home+jobs&skin=corporate&t=all	WORK FROM HOME	SEARCH DIRECTORY
262	http://www.squidoo.com/search/results?q=work+at+home+jobs#q=work+at+home+jobs	WORK FROM HOME	SEARCH DIRECTORY
263	http://www.aerotek.com/searchresults.aspx?kw=work+from+home+jobs	WORK FROM HOME	STAFFING DIRECTORY
264	http://www.net-temps.com/webapps/search/jobs.do?searchTerms=work+at+home&searchvar_textLoc=SC	WORK FROM HOME	STAFFING DIRECTORY
265	http://magazine-agent.com/sub.info/	AFFILIATE	SELL MAGAZINES
266	http://www.amsafone.com/careers/	CALL CENTER	ON-LINE
267	http://www.callcenteroptions.com/careers.asp	WORK@HOME	ON-LINE
268	http://www.dexcomm.com/join-our-team/	CUSTOMER SERVICE	800*252*5552
269	http://www.gecallcentercareers.com/	GENERAL ELECTRIC CALL CENTER	ON-LINE
270	http://www.interpeller.com/jobs.html	CUSTOMER SERVICE REP	ON-LINE

#	URL	Position	Method
271	https://www.google.com/search?q=live+agent+co+uk+become&channel=linkdoctor	LIVE AGENT	ON-LINE SEARCH
272	http://www.lunarpages.com/information/employment/customer-service-representative-I	CSR	ON-LINE
273	http://www.csr-net.com/jointeam.htm	INBOUND CALLERS AND EVALUATORS	ON-LINE
274	http://www.calldesk.com/index.php	VIRTUAL RECEPTIONIST SUBMIT RESUME	CLICK ON CAREERS AND JOIN CALL DESK
275	http://www.bluezebraappointmentsetting.com/Careers.aspx	APPOINTMENT SETTING	ON-LINE
276	http://www.simplyhired.com/k-telephone-appointment-setter-l-tampa-fl-jobs.html	APPOINTMENT SETTING	ON-LINE SEARCH
277	http://jobsearch.money.cnn.com/work-from-home-appointment-setting-telemarketing-jobs-Q0,47.html	APPOINTMENT SETTING	ON-LINE SEARCH
278	http://www.glassdoor.com/job-listing/awesome-appointment-setters-needed-sds-appointments-JV_IC1154429_KO0,34_KE35,51.htm?jl=948209869&paoIdKey=NDA=	SDS APPOINTMENT SETTING	ON-LINE
279	http://working-from-home.jobamatic.com/a/jobs/find-jobs/q-Appointment+Setters+Needed	APPOINTMENT SETTING	SEARCH DIRECTORY
280	http://public.expertbizdev.com/	APPOINTMENT SETTING	BUSINESS DIRECTORY
281	http://www.extendedpresence.com/current-opportunities.html	APPOINTMENT SETTING	ON-LINE SEARCH
282	http://www.nyclimo5.com/careers.htm	CAR SERVICE - DISPATCHER	877-695-4665 DOWNLOAD APPLICATION
283	http://www.jlodge.com/careers/	CSR - MONITORING	ON-LINE
284	http://kowaline.com/opportunity_0206_MonSup.htm	CONSULTANT - MONITORING SUPERVISOR - DATA ANALYST	ON-LINE
285	http://onpointathome.com/opportunities/	COMMUNICATORS - WRITERS	ON-LINE
286	http://fonemed.com/employment	NURSE - TELEPHONE TRIAGE	ON-LINE
287	http://www.advanis.ca/Corporate/Careers	HOME BASED TELEPHONE RESEARCH INTERVIEWER	ON-LINE
288	http://www.serverpoint.com/cu/about/careers.p.html	CSR - TECHNICAL SUPPORT LEVEL 1	ON-LINE
289	http://www.bsgclearing.com/contact_us/careers/live-operator-independent-contractor	VERIFICATION SERVICES	ON-LINE
290	http://www.virtualassistantjobs.com/directory	VIRTUAL ASSISTANT	SEARCH DIRECTORY
291	http://www.theappointmentbiz.com/subcontractors.html	APPOINTMENT SETTER	resume@theappointment.biz.com
292	http://sunlarkresearch.com/Work-for-Us.php	INDEPENDENT COURT RESEARCHERS	ON-LINE
293	http://www.procardinternational.com/careers/index.aspx	ASSOCIATE - AFFILIATE	ON-LINE
294	resume: jobs@pioneerstaffing.com	WORK@HOME	E-MAIL

295	http://www.deltadocument.co/abstractors/	MORTGAGE INDUSTRY	ON-LINE
296	http://nextjobathome.com/job-search-results.php	WORK@HOME	ON-LINE
297	http://www.betheboossnetwork.com/gtim-directory	WORK@HOME	ON-LINE DIRECTORY
298	http://www.cashcrate.com/	SURVEY	ON-LINE
299	http://www.ejury.com/	MOCK TRIALS	ON-LINE
300	GETCUSTOMERSERVICEJOBS.COM	CSR - CALL CENTER	ON-LINE

WORK FROM HOME DIRECTORY

	COMPANY	Status	HOW TO APPLY
1	MEDICAL HOME-BASED	CURRENT	http://cpr-tech.com
2		CURRENT	http://www.advancedb.com
3		CURRENT	http://amphionmedical.com
4		CURRENT	http://www.completetranscriptionservices.com/jobs.html
5		CURRENT	http://www.aetna.com/about-aetna-insurance/aetna-careers/find-a-career/index.html
6		CURRENT	http://www.codebusters.com
7		CURRENT	http://conifechealth.com/careers
8		CURRENT	http://www.diversifiedtyping.com
9		CURRENT	https://external-healthfirst.icims.com/jobs/intro?branding=&mobile=false&width=650&height=500&bga=true&needsRedirect=false
10		CURRENT	http://www.ivhmds.com
11		CURRENT	http://www.accuratetyping.net
12		CURRENT	http://www.mtjobs.com
13		CURRENT	http://www.spectramedi.com
14		CURRENT	http://www.scribeatty.com/web/index.php
15		CURRENT	http://mmodal.com
16		CURRENT	http://www.mtcompmed.com
17		CURRENT	http://www.phoenixmed.com/requirements.htm
18		CURRENT	http://www.professionalmedservices.org/mt_requirements.html
19		CURRENT	http://www.precyse.com
20		CURRENT	http://www.stenomed.com/careers.htm

WORK FROM HOME DIRECTORY

	COMPANY	Status	HOW TO APPLY
1	MYSTERY SHOPPING	Current***	http://www.mysteryshop.org/
2		Current	http://www.apartmentmysteryshopper.com
3		Current	http://www.customerimpactinfo.com/app/webroot/mobile/?url=http%3A%2F%2Fwww.customerimpactinfo.com%2F
4		Current	http://beyondhello.com
5		Current	http://www.worldalliance-retail.org
6		Current	http://www.anothersexposure.us/Job0rs.htm
7		Current	http://www.confervine.com/shoppers-center/become-a-shopper/
8		Current	http://www.performalogics.com/japers.php
9		Current	http://www.woodsgroupinc.com/shoppers/ind_es.php
10		Current	http://teleperusse.com/work_at_home_jobs_telephone.html
11		Current	http://www.strategicevaluations.ca
12		Current	http://www.serviceconnectionsinc.com/shoppe erExpectations.html

WORK FROM HOME DIRECTORY

	COMPANY	Status	HOW TO APPLY
1	Non-Phone Positions	Current	www.talk2rep.com
2		Current	www.sitestaff.com
3		Current	www.needle.com
4		Current	http://cclive.com/gallup_jobs.htm
5		Current	http://www.televated.com
6		Current	http://www.apple.com/jobs/us/aha.html
7		Current	http://www.postloop.com
8		Current	http://www.paperlesspipeline.com
9		Current	http://www.capitaltyping.com/live-chat-support
10		Current	https://www.google.com/about/careers/search/#!t=jo&jid=43087&
11		Current	http://www.asofstone.com/en/company/care er/career.aspx?id=careers
12		Current	http://www.admissionsconsultants.com/empl oyment.asp
13		Current	https://www.liveperson.com/registration/exp ert-registration/expert-signup.aspx
14		Current	http://www.pearsonassessments.com/careers.html
15		Current	http://www.aim4a.com/tutors.php
16		Current	http://recruit.tutor.com/program/index.asp
17		Current	http://www.brainfuse.com/register/becometut or.asp
18		Current	http://www.5tutor.com
19		Current	https://brainmass.com/join-expert
20		Current	https://www.jobsforeathome.com/get/public /home
21		Current	http://www.lionbridge.com/careers
22		Current	http://www.bespacific/adstan/workers/jobs_opportunities/job/Internet-crowd-workers_us/?orisearch=1
23		Current	https://www.mturk.com/mturk/searchbar?sel ectedSearchType=hitgroups&searchWords=cr owdsource&minReward=0.00&x=0&y=0
24		Current	http://www.appen.com/careers
25		Current	http://www.triviawars.com/writers.html
26		Current	http://www.buzzone.com/opportunities.html
27		Current	http://www.ets.org/scoring_opportunities
28		Current	http://www.clickwork.com/indexjsp
29		Current	https://www.mindswarms.com/consumers/ne w?from=kindOfUser&text=Get+paid+for+ans wers&cs=Conduct+research
30		Current	http://videobreak.com/video-videos/
31		Current	http://support.crowdsource.com/support/ho me?retcvr=cloudcrowd
32		Current	https://www.crisinants-content.com/area/register-author.htm
33		Current	http://www.clickworker.com/become-a-clickworker/?utm_source=29435&utm_cam

			paign=CW4CW&utm_medium=email
34		Current	https://www.createspace.com
35		Current	https://www.writeraccess.com/apply-writer
36		Current	http://www.pulsecontent.com/write_for_us.p hp
37		Current	https://www.onlinewritingjobs.com/new-general-signup/
38		Current	http://typists.quicktate.com/transcribers/sign_up

WORK FROM HOME DIRECTORY

	COMPANY	Status	HOW TO APPLY
1	TECHNICAL SUPPORT	CURRENT	http://accoladesupport.com/techjob.html
2		CURRENT	http://www.apple.com/jobs/us/aha.html
3		CURRENT	http://www.dell.com/learn/us/en/uscorp1/co_rp-comm/cr-diversity-wf-flexible-work
4		CURRENT	http://careers.convergys.com
5		CURRENT	http://www.computerassistant.com
6		CURRENT	http://www.arisediogic.com
7		CURRENT	http://geeksontime.com/techs
8		CURRENT	http://www.mcafee.com/about/jobs
9		CURRENT	http://careers.joelonsoftware.com/jobs
10		CURRENT	http://advisctech.com/company-2/career-opportunities
11		CURRENT	http://www.drivengide.com
12		CURRENT	http://www.sitel.com/our-company/media-center/
13		CURRENT	http://www.teletechjobs.com/athome_en-US
14		CURRENT	http://www.apply.worktehome.com/index.htm

WORK FROM HOME DIRECTORY

	COMPANY	Status	HOW TO APPLY
1	TRANSCRIPTION	Current	https://castingwords.com
2		Current	http://mmodal.com/about-us/careers/clinical-documentation-opportunities
3		Current	http://www.productiontranscripts.com/jobs.php
4		Current	http://www.1888typeitup.com/transcription-jobs
5		Current	http://www.allegiscommunicationsinc.coursehost.com/Groups/Config/Home6.asp?LID=1Kx3=d_BPDiQVRgH7D5PRUmI_DgH7RV7OTU_vz
6		Current	http://www.focusfwd.com
7		Current	http://verbalink.com/about-verival-ink/verbal-ink-jobs
8		Current	http://www.2ndtranscription.com/career.aspx
9		Current	http://www.executranglobal.com
10		Current	http://www.callevo.com
11		Current	https://www.speechpad.com/worker
12		Current	http://birchcreekcommunications.com/wp/_auth.html
13		Current	https://www.mturk.com/mturk/welcome

WORK FROM HOME DIRECTORY

	COMPANY	Status	HOW TO APPLY
1	VIRTUAL ASSISTANTS	Current	http://www.vrsoffice.com/subs/subsignup.htm
2		Current	http://virtualteampros.com/
3		Current	http://www.theappointmentbiz.com/subcontractors.html
4		Current	http://www.office88.com/job.htm
5		Current	http://www.contemporaryva.com/home
6		Current	https://www.fancyhands.com/jobs
7		Current	http://www.communityroundtable.com/
8		Current	http://my365assistant.com/
9		Current	http://www.virtualofficesva.com/
10		Current	http://be-a-virtual-assistant.tinyerr.com/portal/apply-now
11		Current	https://www.zirtual.com
12		Current	http://www.assistantmatch.com/asthads.cgi?Publiobs
13		Current	http://www.arise.com
14		Current	http://www.bluezebraappointmentsetting.com/Careers.aspx
15		Current	http://edegreeadvisor.com/jobs/customer-service-representative
16		Current	https://needadesupport.com/help.jb.html
17		Current	http://www.cruise.com/cruise_information/employment.asp?skin=001&pin=&phone=888-555-3116
18		Current	http://www.lionone.com/MainInfo.asp?ProfileID=23388&LocID=56848&BL_ID=30
19		Current	http://www.hsnjobs.com/career.asp
20		Current	http://www.alpine.com/careers
21		Current	http://www.kellyservices.us/US/Careers/Kelly_Connect/Kelly_At_Home/#.Uy4ZtcyDCU
22		Current	https://www.citel.com/careers/work-home/
23		Current	https://hub2-sykes.icims.com/jobs/search?hashed=0&mobile=false&width=698&height=400&bga=true&needsRedirect=false
24		Current	http://www.hipporline.com/athome-en-US
25		Current	http://timecommunications.biz/company/employment
26		Current	http://www.virtalad.net/job_opportunities.htm
27		Current	http://www.aspirelifestyles.com/careers-in-concierge/splash=true
28		Current	https://www.workingsolutions.com/content-home-agents/
29		Current	http://www.myvact.com/jobs/jobs-list.asp
30		Current	http://www.support.com/about/careers/open_jps
31		Current	http://www.agent24.com/content/publiccontent.aspx?PageID=84
32		Current	http://www.ventureloop.com/ventureloop/job_detail.php?ref_hit&jobIds=28891
33		Current	www.directathomejobs.com

34		Current	www.cratyslist.com
35		Current	https://www.aeddirect.com
36		Current	https://www.alpineaccess.com
37		Current	http://join.liveops.com/being-an-agent
38		Current	https://asurionathome.com
39		Current	https://nevasurion.taleo.net/careersection/ncw_ext_banu_cci/jobsearch.ftl?lang=en
40		Current	https://www.odesk.com/virtualassistant

Search Sites (Home Business Opportunities/Work From Home Jobs)
http://www.simplyhired.com/
http://www.careerbuilder.com/Jobseeker/Jobs/JobResults.aspx?IPath=QH&q b=1&s_rawwords=work+at+home+jobs&s_freeloc=SC&s_jobtypes=ALLhttp s://www.linkedin.com/nhome/
http://www.indeed.com/jobs?q=work+from+home&l=SChttp://www.jobsinyourarea.com/
http://www.bing.com/search?q=Home+Business+Opportunities&go=&qs=n&_form=QBRE&pq=home+business+opportunities&sc=8-27&sp=-1&sk=&ghc=1
http://www.tryasi.com/
http://www.bizymoms.com/
http://www.wahm.com/
http://www.linkedup.com/
http://search.about.com/?q=work+from+home+jobs
http://search.aarp.org/browse?Ntt=work+at+home+jobs
http://www.ehow.com/search.html?s=work+at+home+jobs&skin=corporate&_t=all
http://www.squidoo.com/search/results?q=work+at+home+jobs#q=work+at+_home+jobs
http://www.staffmark.com/jobSearch/jobSearch.asp?search=work+from+ho_me+jobs&categoryID=&locationID=&x=57&y=13
http://www.aerotek.com/searchresults.aspx?kw=work+from+home+jobs
http://www.net-temps.com/webapps/search/jobs.do?searchTerms=work+at+home&searchvar_textLoc=SC
http://www.careeronestop.org/reemployment/jobsearch/jobsearchresults.aspx?keyword=work%20at%20home&location=SC&radius=25
SEARCH SITES

TRUCK DISPATCH DIRECTORY

"Online load boards are a great way to help keep your wheels turning so you never have to deadhead. Some load boards are among the oldest websites in the trucking industry. A trucker's network is his most valuable asset and frequenting a reliable load board can be a great way to meet brokers and find work where you otherwise wouldn't be looking. Most of the time all you need is a MC# (Motor Carrier Number) or DOT # depending on if you are looking for loads or providing them" (Raney'sBlog, 2013).

"The big question then becomes: How do I know which load board to trust and how much is too much as far as fees are concerned? Many drivers won't get out of bed for less than $2.00 a mile while others don't seem to mind. It is all about finding the finding a place that consistently offers freight tailored to your schedule, equipment and desired rates" (Raney'sBlog, 2013).

Where to start (Raney'sBlog, 2013)?

"Let's look at some reviews and analysis from across the web of different load boards. We'll compare size, average rates and user feedback. Because freight rates can vary so much from week to week, we'll be trying to aim for averages. There will obviously be exceptionally bad and good loads to find on all of the load boards so we don't suggest using this information to rule out a company completely" (Raney'sBlog, 2013).

DAT Load-board – "The largest load board on the web, and in many respects, the most useful. They have frequently updated freight trends available on their site as well as a large list of driver resources. Another plus is DAT will guarantee payment and help collect in the event on non-payment. They have a free reporting tool to get estimates on their rates averaged by region, weekly. For example, they are reporting that Memphis is averaging $2.15 a mile while Atlanta is at $1.94 a mile" (Raney'sBlog, 2013).

Getloaded.com – "One of the most streamlined boards, Get Loaded is tailored primarily to drivers who quickly need to find load. They have a very high rated mobile app for both I-Phones and Android phones. Their basic package is $29.99 but it doesn't include many features that most truckers desire. You'll have to go to a more premium plan if you want credit scores, back-haul links, and toll information. There are also some questionable reviews on this site concerning the site" (Raney'sBlog, 2013).

TruckStop.com – "Also called the Internet Truck-stop, this load-board has been around since 1995 and charges $35.00 a month for its services. The site is a bit out-dated, but from what we've read online the loads are fine. You will also have to pay for credit checks on brokers at a clip of $15 per 25 checks" (Raney'sBlog, 2013).

123Loadboard.com – "Another board with a good reputation and useful features such as their Rate Check". According to 123Loadboard.com (Raney'sBlog, 2013):

"Picking smarter loads and using the rate check tool is definitely part of remaining profitable in this industry. For the best results, it seems good to mix the rate matching tools of different load boards and compare the regions you'd be most interested in. Many times the advertised price will not be what the freight left the dock for so make sure to establish terms with reputable brokers" (Raney'sBlog, 2013).

"There are load boards popping up on the internet all the time so make sure to never settle for a sub-par service. The monthly fees can add up so make sure to look for promotional offers and free trials. Here is a list of a few trials you could get started with" (Raney'sBlog, 2013):

1. 10 days free at 123loadboard.com
2. 10 days free at getloaded.com
3. 30 days free at truckersedge.net
4. 30 days free at transcore.com

"The internet is here to stay and is quickly becoming the beset and fastest way to do business in the trucking industry. If you are an owner/operator, make sure to make online load boards part of your business model moving forward. Even if they are not a primary source of leads and revenue it is always a good idea to have a backup plan for when times are slow. With some boards costing nothing, or next to nothing, what do you have to lose" (Raney'sBlog, 2013)?

	COMPANY	Status	HOW TO APPLY
1	RIGHT NOW LOADS	CURRENT	http://www.rightnowloads.com/
			888-852-4238
2	123 LOAD BOARD	CURRENT	http://www.123loadboard.com/
		MOST USED	877-875-5301
3	UShip	CURRENT	http://www.uship.com/
			support@uship.com
4	INTERNET TRUCK STOP	CURRENT	http://www.truckstop.com/Classifieds/Classified_s.aspx
		MOST USED	800-203-2540
5	DIRECT FREIGHT	CURRENT	http://www.directfreight.com/home/
			888-894-4198
6	DAT	CURRENT	http://www.dat.com/LandingPages/ppcmini/home.aspx?cid=201202_cpc_google_loadfinder&_gclid=CN-8-4bq97oCFepFMgodzy8Anw
		MOST USED	800-551-8847
7	INTERSTATE CAPITAL	CURRENT	http://www.interstatecapital.com/factoring_industries/transportation-distribution
			800-422-0766
8	THE SUPER BOARD	CURRENT	http://www.thesuperboard.com/search-_freight/find-loads-now.cfm
			877-730-1942

9	GET LOADED	CURRENT	https://www.getloaded.com/packages/trucker?
		MOST USED	888-565-3921
10	TRUCK DRIVER JOBS 411	CURRENT	http://www.truckdriverjobs411.com/
		FREE JOB BOARD	800-937-8785
11	1099 TRUCKER	CURRENT	http://www.1099trucker.com/
			(888) 830-2326
12	CLASSIFIED DRIVERS	CURRENT	http://www.classadrivers.com/forum/owner-operators-forums/34808-brokers-getting-loads-new-owner-operator.html
		FREE FORUM	USE ONLINE MESSAGE BOARD
13	ATS	CURRENT	http://www.ats-sureway.com/find-truck-loads.html
		LARGEST NETWORK	800-338-0497
14	INDEED.COM	CURRENT	http://www.indeed.com/jobs?q=LOADS+FOR+OWNER+OPERATORS&l=SOUTH+CAROLINA
		FREE SEARCH	LOADS FOR OWNER OPERATORS
15	LAYOVER	CURRENT	http://www.layover.com/owneroperator/
	USED BY J.B. HUNT		APPLY ON-LINE
16	CARRIER CENTRAL	CURRENT	http://www.carriercentral.com/load_results.php
			1-888-765-2825
17	VESSAGE	CURRENT	http://www.vessage.com/
			CONTACT ON-LINE VIA E-MAIL
18	BUBBA JUNK.COM	CURRENT	http://www.bubbajunk.com/search/g-owner-operator-driving-jobs/
		FREE SEARCH	TRUCKING JOBS
19	OWNER OPERATOR JOB	FREE SEARCH	http://www.owneroperatorjob.com/
20	GLOBAL TRANZ FREIGHT BROKER / DISPATCH	CURRENT	http://www.globaltranz.com/freight-agent-program?gclid=CI-9gpjz97oCFY5FMgodgh0ApA

WHAT OWNER OPERATORS ARE TO EXPECT?

TRAILERS REQUIRED FOR TRANSPORT:

1. FLAT BED
2. STEPDECK
3. FLAT BED WITH TARPS
4. VANS
5. REEFER
6. SD

INFORMATION REQUIRED BY COMPANIES:

- MC "MOTOR CARRIER" ID# IS REQUIRED FOR OUT-OF-STATE
- W-9 FORM
- PROOF OF INSURANCE
- BACKGROUND CHECK
- AGREEMENT FOR SERVICES FORM
- DISPATCH SERVICE AUTHORIZATION FORM
- COMPANY PROFILE FORM
- DEBIT OR CREDIT CARD AUTHORIZATION FORM

MOTOR CARRIER NUMBER

CONTACT LOCAL:

- U.S. DEPT. OF TRANSPORTATION
- THE FEDERAL MOTOR CARRIER SAFETY ADMINISTRATION

OWN YOUR OWN FREIGHT BROKERAGE / TRANSPORTATION BUSINESS

"DIANA'Z HOUSE, INC. CAN SHOW YOU HOW!"

What is this opportunity?

With this opportunity, you will own your own Transportation and Logistics business while partnering with other companies. In addition, Diana'z House, Inc. can show you how to handle all of the back-end office work including: invoicing, receivables, credit, collections, claims, obtaining Customer Specific Pricing, and of course top-notch support. You can receive a minimum of 50% of the profit for LTL shipments with unlimited earnings potential. You are paid twice per month on invoiced shipments. In essence, the company or companies you contract with will pay you before the money is collected from the customer (Tranz, 2013).

This entrepreneurial model works because Agents use a consultative approach and leverage out competitive pricing and highly technological ways of managing freight. Your focus as an Agent is to obtain and maintain customers while building equity in your own company. This program has been proven by over 200 freight sales professionals nationwide (Tranz, 2013).

If you are an experienced freight or logistics sales professional, you are Freight Broker Agent material.

Requirement #1 - Agents MUST have a minimum of 2 years of freight sales (broker school does not qualify)

Requirement #2 - Agents MUST have a current book of business/relationships with multiple shippers (Tranz, 2013).

You'll make an additional:

$1,000 per month

$12,000 per year

$36,000 over 3 years

REFERENCES

Dictionary.Com. (2014, April 28). Promissory Note. Retrieved from Dictionary.Com: http://legal-dictionary.thefreedictionary.com/Note+(real+estate)

Google, I. (2014, April 26). Google Search. Retrieved from Scam: https://www.google.com/#q=DEFINE+SCAM

Raney'sBlog. (2013, November 22). Semi Truck News and Information. Retrieved from Raney's Blog: http://blog.raneystruckparts.com/trucker-information/what-are-the-best-load-boards-for-owner-operators-lets-find-out/

Tranz, G. (2013, November 22). Frieght Agent Program. Retrieved from GlobalTranz.com: http://www.globaltranz.com/freight-agent-program?gclid=CI-9gpjz97oCFY5FMgodgh0ApA

DIANA'Z HOUSE, INC.

"NEWSCAST"

www.ingramcontent.com/pod-product-compliance
Lightning Source LLC
Chambersburg PA
CBHW080523240526
45472CB00021BA/1993